POLTERS

DEMONS *in the* HOME

CLEANSING YOUR HOME
FROM DEMONIC INTRUDERS

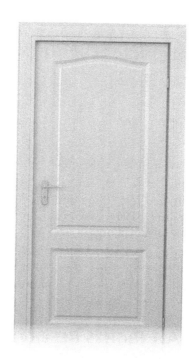

BY FRANK HAMMOND

POLTERGEISTS:
DEMONS IN THE HOME

BY FRANK HAMMOND

ISBN 10: 0-89228-390-4
ISBN 13: 978-089228-390-3

IMPACT CHRISTIAN BOOKS, INC.
332 Leffingwell Ave., Suite 101
Kirkwood, MO 63122
(314) 822-3309

www.impactchristianbooks.com

INTRODUCTION

Do you, or does someone you know, have demonic spirits in the home? Are you thrust out of sleep by banging doors, the sound of footsteps, or lights going on and off? Do you see mysterious shadows on the wall or creatures at the foot of your bed?

If so, I have good news for you. Your house can be cleansed. Just as the inside man can be swept clean of demonic spirits, so too can a house or a dwelling be swept clean from the presence and harassment of evil spirits.

The process of ridding one's house of demonic spirits begins with a careful assessment of the objects and literature we have allowed into our homes. It also encompasses an assessment of who the previous tenants were and what kind of spiritual activity they were up to. It requires a consideration of generational curses, or demons who have been passed down through your bloodline. Ultimately, the deliverance of your home or property from demons mirrors the deliverance of a person from demons — as "whosoever shall call upon the name of the Lord shall be delivered" (Joel 2:32).

MY EXPERIENCE IN
HOTELS, HOSPITALS & CHURCHES

Let me begin by saying I am thoroughly convinced that properties, public buildings, houses and even churches can be inhabited by evil spirits and sometimes need to be cleansed.

As an example, Ida Mae and I have traveled quite extensively in order to minister to people around the United States and abroad. This has required us to stay in a lot of hotels. Early on in our ministry I began to notice that I would have terrible dreams when staying in some of those places. I remember in one instance, a scene passed through my mind, during a dream, in which someone with a rifle was killing people randomly. When I awoke, I felt so unclean. And I wondered, "Why would I have a dream like that?"

Right at that moment, the Spirit of the Lord spoke to me and impressed upon me the word "television." People who had stayed in that room previously had watched violent movies on cable television, and this attracted violent spirits to those rooms. Do you know what we found out? Once we cleansed that room there were no more problems with nightmares. Praise the Lord!

After that, we learned to do this as part of a routine. When we go into a hotel room, the first thing we do is cleanse it, and claim it as property of the kingdom of God.

In another instance, we visited a church in southern

California, and it was in a pretty rough part of town. The pastor informed us that he had booked us into the nicest hotel in the area. Well, when we arrived the first thing I noticed was the sign outside advertising "hourly rates." So, immediately we knew what kind of hotel this was. When arrived in our room, we found that there were mirrors on all the walls and on the ceiling as well. So we knew that place needed to be cleansed!

This is also true of hospitals. Things happen in hospital rooms and operating rooms, like trauma, suffering, pain and death. I learned quickly that when either Ida Mae or I had to stay in a hospital, we would need to spiritually cleanse the room. We would establish that the room was part of the kingdom of God, and any spirit that was contrary to, or hated, the operation of God's kingdom, had to go! We commanded every spirit drawn to that room, because of suffering, pain, death or trauma, to leave and pronounced that they had no right to remain.

I also prayed over every blood transfusion given to Ida Mae, because spirits can indwell the blood. The Bible tells us that "For the life of the flesh is in the blood" (Lev. 17:11), so we know the importance of blood and the spiritual nature of things behind it. I stood against any transference of spirits through blood transfusions.

It is just sensible that when we go into someone else's territory, and it is going to be a residence for a while, that we claim that area as part of God's kingdom and cleanse those places from demonic spirits.

We have even sensed a demonic presence when entering into

churches. There is sometimes a heaviness, a spiritual oppression, when we walk into a church and we sense it immediately. So, at times, we need to cleanse church buildings as well. Once in our own church, the Lord gave me discernment, and revealed that there was a "stifling spirit" that had lodged itself in our fellowship. So when I took to the podium, I took authority over it. Up to that point we had been really struggling in our praise and worship of God. The whole situation turned around almost instantly when we got rid of that spirit that was stifling the praise and worship of God. The power of God does work!

So, if you are struggling or up against a hindrance, or some type of oppression, don't second guess it. If you have any suspicion that it could be a spirit, go ahead and challenge it. When people tell me that they don't know whether they have a specific demon or not, I say "when in doubt, cast it out." It is better to challenge something that is not there than not to challenge something that is there. Nothing will be harmed if you challenge something that is not present, but if something is present, it is going to have to go when you use the authority of the Name of Jesus.

Spiritual Doors
into the Home

There are various doors that can be opened in the spiritual realm to allow demon spirits to enter and indwell a property. Some of the major openings include idolatry, the occult and familiar spirits, and they can all overlap. The general term used for a spirit that causes disturbances in homes and properties is "poltergeist." This is a German word, where "polter" means *noisy*, and "geist" is the term for *spirit* or *ghost*. The term literally means "noisy ghost." One of the common manifestations of the poltergeist spirit is that it makes noises.

I have learned over the years that some of the ghost stories we hear about have some credence to them. The old lines about "I heard chains rattling," or "I heard footsteps on the stairs," or even "I saw shadows against the wall" prove true in some cases. We have heard from people about how glass shatters out of nowhere and hits the floor, or a light turns on and off, or doors and cabinets open and shut. Weird things can happen like that in houses where there are poltergeist spirits.

Several years ago, we were ministering to a fellowship in Texas, and a lady invited us to minister in her home. Before we went, she informed us that there was one area in a bedroom in that house that was always cold. It was an area of about 3 feet square. You could put your hand on that hardwood floor anytime in the year, including the hot Texas months of summer, and no matter how warm the temperature was in the room, that spot was always cold. She had also seen spirits. From her bedroom, she could see down the hallway and from time to time a demon would manifest, a dwarf spirit. When it would turn to enter a room, from a sideways vantage point, it looked like plate glass.

So we wondered what gave that spirit the right to enter that home. It turns out that this woman's grandfather had lived with them for a while and he was involved in occult practices. He had actually died in that bedroom. So in this case, we knew some keys to unlock the spiritual conditions in that house, and after we cleansed that property and commanded those spirits to get out of that house, all those problems ended. The spirit had left!

The operating principle behind poltergeist spirits is that they come into a home to cause fear, to harass and to hinder the lives of the inhabitants.

Remember this one spiritual principle: a spirit cannot be anywhere unless it has a *legal right*. This is true of personal deliverance and it is also true of houses harassed by demonic spirits. In other words, a demon cannot just latch onto you, or enter into your life, for no reason. You cannot just walk down the street, bump into a demon, and acquire one — it does not work that way. Demons come into our lives via sin doors. It could be a sin that was committed somewhere back in an ancestral line, by parents, grandparents or great grandparents, and the curse of that sin is being passed down to consecutive generations. Or it could be a result of sin in our own lives. It could even be sin from the prior tenant.

This is an important point. When you go to cleanse someone of demons, there are certain conditions that person has to meet or those demons do not have to leave. Or if they do leave, they can come back seven times worse (Luke 11:26). A good example of that principle is in Matthew 18 where Jesus is talking about forgiveness. He said that if we bear resentment, bitterness or hatred toward anybody, that gives an evil spirit the legal right to torment us.

So, if some act or condition or idol has invited a spirit into a house, the same principle holds true. As long as that sinful behavior, idol, or occult activity, continues in the home, the demon has a legal right to stay and you cannot make him leave. He will have a legal right to be there until the idol is removed, and the occult activity, or other types of sinful pursuits, are ceased and repented of. This principle applies whether it is a person, a house, a piece of land, a public building or even a church. Some activity or some object has given that spirit a right to be there.

If there is anything present that pertains to the demonic kingdom, the demons have a legal right to indwell that property.

When we first started our traveling ministry years ago, we met a man who reported that he had poltergeist spirits in his home. He told us what led him to look for help. One night he heard a racket and it startled him. As he sat up in bed he saw a hairy human hand sticking through his window in his bedroom.

The first question I ask in those situations is "Who lived here previously?" In other words, who was the previous owner or tenant? If you know who that was and what kind of person he or she was, that will often provide a key as to why that spirit is in that property. He said, "It is a brand new home, we had it built ourselves." So, it could not have been a previous owner.

As we prayed about the situation, the Lord gave us a *word of knowledge* and revealed the source of that thing. I received a simple word from the Lord: "Occult literature." So I asked this man if he had any occult literature, and I began to name a number of possibilities: Freemasonic or Rosicrucian literature, Christian Scientist literature, etc. And he said, "Well, yes, my mother was a Christian scientist. She died not long ago and we cleaned out her house and found a lot of literature. I put it into a box, and I stored it in the attic of my house."

I asked him if he was willing to get the literature out of his home, and he agreed. He threw it away and then we walked through his house, cleansing each room and commanding those spirits to leave. Praise the Lord, that was the end of his problem!

IDOLATRY: A COMMON CAUSE OF SPIRITS IN THE HOME

In Corinthians, Paul provides a lecture for us on the evils of idolatry.

> **Wherefore, my dearly beloved, flee from idolatry.**
> **1 Corinthians 10:14**

Paul says "flee" from things considered idols, run away from such things. The sense is that we are to get as far away as quickly as possible from anything idolatrous.

> **The cup of blessing which we bless, is it not the communion of the blood of Christ? The bread which we break, is it not the communion of the body of Christ?**
> **1 Corinthians 10:16**

The Greek word for "communion" is *koinonia* which means fellowship. He says here that when you partake of the Lord's Supper you are fellowshipping with one another, *and* you are fellowshipping with Jesus. This is the background for what he is about to say next.

Behold Israel after the flesh: are not they which eat of the sacrifices partakers of the altar?

1 Corinthians 10:18

So they are bonded together, there is a relationship there, a *koinonia* between God and the ones eating the sacrifice.

What say I then? that the idol is any thing, or that which is offered in sacrifice to idols is any thing?

But I say, that the things which the Gentiles sacrifice, they sacrifice to devils [demons], and not to God: and I would not that ye should have fellowship with devils [demons].

1 Corinthians 10:19–20

Do you see the carryover of the idea of fellowship that Paul is using here when he compares the altar of the Lord to idolatry? Both involve fellowship. Both involve *koinonia*, but the Gentiles who fellowship with idols are in fact fellowshipping with demons. When the heathens worship idols, they are fellowshipping with demons; that is what happens when you get involved with idolatry. In other words, you cannot have idolatry and not have demons! You cannot participate in idolatry without participating with demons.

Ye cannot drink the cup of the Lord, and the cup of devils [demons]: ye cannot be partakers of the Lord's table, and of the table of devils [demons]. Do we provoke the Lord to jealousy? are we stronger than he?

1 Corinthians 10:21–22

Paul tells us that we cannot mix our worship of God with the worship of demons. We cannot worship God in a true way in spirit and in truth while mixing that with idolatry. God is a jealous God and He will not tolerate that.

GOD SPEAKS AGAINST IDOLATRY

Let's see what happened when God first gave the commandments to Moses.

Thou shalt not make unto thee any graven image, or any likeness of any thing that is in heaven above, or that is in the earth beneath, or that is in the water under the earth.

Ex 20:4

We are not to make any representation of any created thing to represent the almighty God that we are worshiping and serving. Continuing on in Exodus 20:5,

> **Thou shalt not bow down thyself to them, nor serve them: for I the LORD thy God am a jealous God, visiting the iniquity of the fathers upon the children unto the third and fourth generation of them that hate me...**

Again, we see that God is a jealous God. If we disobey this commandment, it is the same as if we "hate" God as it says here.

In Ex. 34, God is giving instructions to His people as they prepare to enter the promised land, Canaan. Canaan is a land filled with idol worshipers. God warns His people to not get involved in idolatry. He implores them to destroy everything that pertains to idolatry of the inhabitants because if they don't, it would become a snare and be a source of contamination to Israel. We are to keep ourselves separate from idol worship.

> **Take heed to thyself, lest thou make a covenant with the inhabitants of the land whither thou goest, lest it be for a snare in the midst of thee:**
>
> **But ye shall destroy their altars, break their images, and cut down their groves:**
>
> **For thou shalt worship no other god: for the LORD, whose name is Jealous, is a jealous God...**
>
> Ex 34:12–14

Even God's name, apparently, means "jealous."

Let me give you a simple understanding of what idolatry is. When someone becomes involved in idolatry, he or she is going to a source other than God to receive the things that only God should give. If you go to a source other than God seeking wisdom, knowledge, guidance or power, you have entered into idolatry.

We think about idolatry in African or South American cultures, but not so much in America. Yet there is idolatry in our midst; it is a worldwide condition.

> **Take ye therefore good heed unto yourselves; for ye saw no manner of similitude on the day that the LORD spake unto you in Horeb out of the midst of the fire...**
>
> **Deut 4:15**

Moses is talking about when God spoke to him on Mt. Sinai, where there was the cloud, lightning and trumpets' blast. He is saying "You did not see any form; God did not appear in any form that you could draw a picture of."

> **Lest ye corrupt yourselves, and make you a graven image, the similitude of any figure, the likeness of male or female, The likeness of any beast that is on the earth, the likeness of any winged fowl that flieth in the air, The likeness of any thing that creepeth on the ground, the**

likeness of any fish that is in the waters beneath the earth: And lest thou lift up thine eyes unto heaven, and when thou seest the sun, and the moon, and the stars, even all the host of heaven, shouldest be driven to worship them, and serve them, which the LORD thy God hath divided unto all nations under the whole heaven.

Deut 4:16–19

In relationship to God, there is not to be any kind of image or picture that represents the Father, Son or Holy Spirit. The Holy Spirit is not a bird. Amen? God chose not to give any description whatsoever of Jesus. I find that interesting. It would be like a husband cutting out a picture of a female model from a magazine and hanging it on the wall and then telling his wife that it was supposed to be a picture of her. That would not go over too well! You can imagine how God would feel about the same thing.

THE LINK BETWEEN SUPERSTITION AND IDOLATRY

Anything that is occult is idolatrous. Divination, fortune telling, Ouija boards, tarot readings, transcendental meditation and other occult practices are all seeking a source of wisdom, knowledge, guidance or power other than God. These are forbidden sources.

Superstition is also idolatry. It is the belief that something or someone will bring you luck.

In one of his missionary journeys, Paul wandered through Athens and noted how many idols he saw along the streets.

Then Paul stood in the midst of Mars' hill, and said, Ye men of Athens, I perceive that in all things ye are too superstitious.

Acts 17:22

In the Amplified Bible, "too superstitious" is translated "very reverent to demons" (APMC). Paul knew their hearts and perceived that they were paying reverence to demonic spirits through their idolatry.

Superstition is a respect for demons. Black cats, Friday the 13th, broken mirrors, stepping on a crack, rabbits feet and other such things are in reality paying homage to the demonic realm.

My mother walked in the light that she had, but she was superstitious. When I was getting married to Ida Mae, I went to pick out a tie for our wedding and it had red in it. When my mother saw that she almost passed out from fear. She said, "You cannot wear that tie because it has red in it. Don't you know it is bad luck to wear red in a wedding? You remember my sister, don't you? She married and three months after her wedding day her husband died of small pox. He wore something red on his wedding day." I told her I understood what she was saying, but I was going to wear that red tie!

Remember that being superstitious is being respectful of demons.

THE SNARES THAT CAUSE US TO KEEP FORBIDDEN OBJECTS IN OUR HOMES

The graven images of their gods shall ye burn with fire: thou shalt not desire the silver or gold that is on them, nor take it unto thee, lest thou be snared therin: for it [the silver and the gold] is an abomination to the LORD thy God. Neither shalt thou bring an abomination into thine house, lest thou be a cursed thing like it: but thou shalt utterly detest it, and thou shalt utterly abhor it; for it is a cursed thing.

Deut. 7:25–26

When you find an idol, do not bring it into your house. We had a lady for years in our fellowship who was dedicated to foreign missions. She spent much of her life in China. When she came back from the mission field, just before she died, she asked me to preach at her funeral — the first funeral I had ever preached. She had brought back from the mission field a life-sized head carved out of wood, which was an idol. She told us that it had at one time had jewels where the eyes were. I finally grew tired of keeping that head and gave it to someone in the neighborhood and to this day I regret that act; I had passed along a source of a curse.

God says to abhor those things, to detest those things, to destroy them.

When we first started traveling in the deliverance ministry, we were at a church in the Midwest. A man in the meeting identified himself as from a specific denomination. He said his job was to go to the mission field and learn about the work and then represent those missions to churches around the country. He commented that he was having trouble in his house, especially with his 14-year-old son. He said his son awakened night after night, and was troubled in his sleep. This boy sensed the presence of something in his bedroom. Since we had been teaching on demons, he asked us to come to his house and cleanse it from any demonic presence.

When we walked into that house, we were stunned. The house was completely loaded with idolatrous artifacts from the mission field. There was a witch's mask over the fireplace and next to it a cow's tail that had been used as a fetish by a witch doctor. On the table, there were little figurines. When we looked closer, we noticed they represented people in various perverse sexual acts.

I said, "No wonder you have been having trouble in this house. No wonder your son is in torment. These artifacts are idolatrous, and you need to destroy them!"

His reply was, "Oh no, missionaries gave those items to me. They are important to me, I am not going to give them up. If the witch's mask bothers you I will put it in the garage while you minister."

I said, "Brother, I don't think we can do much under these circumstances." And we couldn't, we could not resolve anything in that home because there was a legal right for those demons to be there.

There is a follow-up to this story. It so happened that we were ministering 20 years later in Texas and that man showed up at one of our meetings. He asked if we remembered him, from when we tried to minister to his family and his troubled son. He told us that after we had left town, his wife and he talked about it again and decided to get rid of that stuff. So they destroyed all of it, and commanded the spirits out of their home. After that, their son had no more trouble at night and there was a peace about him.

There are things that snare us into keeping things we should not keep. An example would be *sentimentality*. We can become sentimental about pictures, artifacts and various possessions, so much so that we feel pressure to keep them even when the Lord is nudging us to get them out of our house. As an example in my own life, my mother chose me among all the siblings to be the custodian of the family heirlooms. She kept most of them in a cedar chest. When I was grown and married, and would visit, she would show me the cedar chest with all the notes she had written about where the item came from and who gave it to her. Those heirlooms were not important to me, but they were to her and since she was adamant about passing them on, this put the burden on me to perpetuate the keeping of these items. When she passed away, we kept those items in our attic and they moved along with us as we settled in different locations. We were in a kind of bondage with those possessions until they were destroyed in a flood.

You can also become snared by gifts from other people. This is particularly problematic when those people visit and ask where the item is displayed in your home. We are called to make choices about these items, as to whether they are spiritual healthy, spiritually neutral, or spiritually unhealthy.

We can be snared by covetousness and greed. That is what the seventh chapter of Joshua speaks of with regard to the story of Achan. When the people of God went against the city of Jericho, God said that city and its spoil were the first-fruits, such that all the spoil was to be dedicated to God and belong to Him. It was dedicated to God. Achan coveted some of the silver, gold and other possessions he came across when the Israelites were taking the city. He hid them in his tent and this created problems for the camp of Israel, so that when they fought against the smaller city of Ai, they were defeated soundly in battle. Joshua asked God why the defeat took place, and he was told there was sin in the camp. Achan finally confessed to his sin and the camp was cleansed. He had coveted something that was dedicated to the Lord and it thus became a curse.

Anything that is dedicated to God belongs to God. That is the principle that is involved in the tithe. In Malachi 3, the tithe is holy and devoted to God. So if you keep that which is devoted to God out of your own covetousness and greed, then even the blessing can become a curse. The principle at work here is: give to God that which is God's and destroy idols and artifacts that belong to the devil.

The real question that should arise when we are considering what to keep and what to throw out of our homes is: *What does God think about it?* Does this give any legal right to the enemy to come in? What advantage, if any, does it give to Satan?

When I was younger, I had been an avid collector of American Indian artifacts. That was my hobby. I spent a large part of my life exploring for such artifacts in the ranch lands of Northern Texas. God began to deal with me about this. He told me that all the items I had collected were associated with Indian worship and idolatry, and I had to get rid of it.

Throughout the period of my younger years I suffered from severe allergies, primarily asthma and hay fever, from about the age of 11 when I began to collect these artifacts. When I decided to obey the Lord and removed those idolatrous things out of my house, and commanded the spirits related to them to leave, I was healed of my allergies. That was the key to rid myself of the demonic harassment caused by a legal right for the spirits to afflict me. I was living under a type of curse and did not even know it.

In Acts 19, when the sons of Sceva attempted to do what Paul was doing in the casting out of spirits, they were overpowered by the demons. They said:

> And the evil spirit answered and said to them, "I recognize Jesus, and I know about Paul, but who are you?"
>
> Acts 19:15, NASB

This created quite stir and word spread about the authority of the ministry of Paul in Ephesus.

> This became known to all, both Jews and Greeks, who lived in Ephesus; and fear fell upon them all and the name of the Lord Jesus was being magnified... And many of those who practiced magic brought their books together and began burning them in the sight of everyone; and they counted up the price of them and found it fifty thousand pieces of silver. So the word of the Lord was growing mightily and prevailing.
>
> Acts 19:17–20, NASB

That was a pretty valuable collection. Notice their obedience in cleansing themselves from the demonic books in their possession.

I had a ministry friend who had led a man to the Lord. The new believer wanted to make a donation to this friend's ministry as a result and was offering him $1.5 million in artwork. When my friend walked into the house and saw the occult nature of the artwork, he said, "Sir, I can't receive this. This is all idolatrous. All this has a curse on it." And the man said, "Well if it is no good to you then it is probably no good to me too." So he destroyed $1.5 million of his artwork. He had to ask himself what price he was willing to pay to get free from a curse associated with those occult works of art.

Consider
Previous Occupants

When you settle into a new home or residence, consider the previous owners or tenets. Try to be aware of any occult activity that was going on there, ranging from witchcraft, cults, tragic deaths or murders in the house, etc. I became acquainted with a young man and his family a few years ago, and his family came to one of our services. He moved into an apartment and was having trouble sleeping. He told us he had never had trouble sleeping before living in this new residence. He said he could move to the couch in the family room and sleep well, but not in the bedroom itself. I began to explain to him about poltergeist spirits and suggested he begin to cleanse that property. I suggested he take some anointing oil and anoint the door-frames, bedposts, etc. around the house and particularly in the bedroom. I asked, "By the way, do you know who lived in that house before you?" He replied, "Well, I never met the person but I heard it was a woman. She did not leave a forwarding address so some of her mail continues to come to the house; a lot of that stuff was occult literature." So I impressed on him that he needed to command every evil spirit that was attracted to that home to leave that property. Then, he was to bless that property in the Name of Jesus and invite the Holy Spirit to take up residence.

Well, praise God, he did that and got instant results! He was so excited he called me to tell me the good news. He even began to share with the neighbors about what had happened, and how he was set free. The Lord used that experience to open his whole family up to the deliverance ministry and I have had the opportunity to minister to his sisters, his brother-in-law and others. Simply the miracle they saw in him, and the change in his life, drew them to the Lord.

In another instance, I had a preacher friend who moved to start a church in New Mexico. When they moved into their new home they knew something was not right spiritually. His wife said one day she was standing at the sink, washing dishes, and an urge came over her to commit suicide. She said she grabbed the sink and held on till her knuckles turned white to keep herself from going to get her husband's gun. The husband also told me that one night he was awakened and it felt like someone was lifting the covers off his feet. As he began to wake up he tapped his wife to tell her what was going on, and it happened again: as they watched they saw the covers rise up about a foot off his feet and then drop down again.

We found the source of these problems was the prior resident. Apparently there was a pastor who had lived in the house just prior to them moving in. This former resident had left church in the middle of the service and driven to a secluded place and committed suicide. That spirit of suicide was in the house.

They prayed against that spirit and the poltergeist spirit creating havoc in the home, cleansed the house and the problems went away.

VARIOUS PARAPHERNALIA TO CONSIDER

Consider the *toys* and *games* your children have in your home. The toy aisle in the local store can be quite a frightening experience these days. It is amazing what gross, demonic stuff is being offered to our children. Many parents, including mine, never learned to judge those things with spiritual eyes; they never realized that they could be bringing evil spirits into a house in the form of games or toys.

Souvenirs are another example. We have to be very careful what we chose to bring back with us from foreign countries.

Literature is also a dangerous door opener to demons.

Amulets, like the peace symbol, inverted pentagrams, zodiac symbols, or even Indian jewelry can open doors for demonic spirits. Native Americans sometimes perform rituals over their jewelry before they sell it to the public. If this is the case, that is a spiritually dangerous object to bring into your house or to wear on your body.

The Ankh. This is a cross with a loop at the top. That is a symbol that comes out of Egypt, and the dictionary suggests it represents the male and female creative power. In other words, it is a fertility idol, and is meant to honor the gods of fertility in Egypt.

Freemasonic paraphernalia is also a door-opener to

demonic spirits. Often, these objects get passed down through generations without any concept of the demonic presence that goes with them. This includes all the branches of secret societies, not just the Freemasons, as they all tend to have occult origins.

Truly, any objects connected with **witchcraft** or the **occult** could allow entry for a demonic presence.

A few years ago we had a family visit our church and the mother explained that because her grandmother was aged, she was living with them. But the mother had always sensed the grandmother was heavily involved in witchcraft. Her grandmother eventually passed away, and after she died, the family saw apparitions of the grandmother in the house. Also, her grandmother had a favorite chair that she would sit in. After her passing, whenever anyone from the family would sit in that chair their skin would feel pricked, as if with needles. After numerous searches of the chair, and finding nothing sharp, they began to see the connection.

The family asked me and my fellow pastor to go to their house and cleanse it. By the time we arrived, they had already thrown out or destroyed all of the witchcraft paraphernalia that the grandmother had stored at the house. We went through that house with the anointing oil, and anointed every room, wall, door frame, cabinet and closet; I mean the whole thing! We commanded all demonic spirits associated with the grandmother to leave and never return. Then we blessed the house in Jesus' Name and invited the Holy Spirit to set up residence there.

That was the turning point. All the bizarre activity and apparitions ceased after that point. Praise the Lord! Our God is good, and He is far, far greater than the power of demons. He is mighty to save (Zeph. 3:17).

Remember the story of Balaam? The king wanted Balaam to put a curse on the Israelites, but he could not.

We were ministering in the Southeast United States a number of years ago. We were at a small church, and there was a lady attending who was very wealthy. She had just built a new, expensive home. She wanted Ida Mae and I to come and pray over her house and to bless it. When we walked into her house, we found that it was decorated with Chinese dragons and serpents and various idols from the East. Ida Mae, who has always had a tremendous *gift of discernment*, spoke very directly to her and told her we could not bless this house in the condition it was in. The only way, she told her, we could bless this house was for her to remove all the pagan idolatry and spiritual mementos. She refused. She had spent tens of thousands of dollars decorating the house and, unfortunately, could not part with the artwork.

SOME RULES FOR DEALING WITH IDOLS

When you accept of a truth like this, please do not go on a crusade. Do not become obsessed with it. Obsession is not a spiritually healthy condition.

Rather, when you come across idolatry in other people's lives, be respectful. Don't destroy other people's idols. If they ask for your opinion, you can give them your opinion. However, let them do the destroying. Your role is to reveal the truth to them.

Pray over your own property and your own possessions. Then do whatever the Holy Spirit leads you to do.

In some instances, we are simply called to encourage others to pray over their own property. Let them develop some spiritual insight and wisdom, and learn to rely on the Holy Spirit in these matters.

Recognize your spiritual authority in Christ. If something like this happens in your house, address it in the Name of Jesus. You, as a believer, have a part to play and you do not need to be an expert. You do not need to have Brother Frank Hammond along with you, because you have the authority to do this on your own. Sometimes it is good to have someone with you, a fellow believer, to help you discern. However, know that you have the authority to deal with whatever situation the devil is trying to create in your home or property.

Remember these simple steps:

- Destroy everything that gives any right to the devil.

- Walk through and anoint walls and doorways with oil.

- Command every foul spirit to leave.

- Dedicate the place and everyone associated with it to the Lord.

- While we may not know all the sins of our ancestors, and the effect on our bloodline, we do have the authority to break all that garbage in a general sense in Jesus' name. Come against the sins and the effects of those sins, and any demonic curses on the bloodline, in Jesus' name.

How do I pray in this kind of situation? I pray a simple prayer like this:

In the name of Jesus, I speak now to the demons in this place. I do not care what gave you the right to be here, but this is the dwelling place of God.

This is an earthly headquarters for God's kingdom and you have no right to be here.

All the people within this house are given to God, they are dedicated to Him.

I revoke your legal right to be here and I command you demons to go and never return in Jesus' Name.

Lord, forgive all the sins of my family and my ancestors. As for any spirit associated with them that has been passed down through the bloodline, I command it to go in Jesus Name.

We now dedicate this place to the Lord. Holy Spirit, you come in and take control of this place. You rule over this house.

When you eliminate the legal right for demons to occupy a house, like occult literature or idols, and you pray a simple prayer like this, you will get results.

For those of you looking for a more in-depth house cleansing prayer, consider the following:

DELIVERANCE AND HOUSE CLEANING PRAYER

Lord Jesus,

I belong to you. You went to the cross and shed Your blood and died for my sins. You took the penalty of sin that was due to me and bore it yourself. Lord, I accept your sacrifice. By faith I receive your salvation.

You told us in Galatians 3 that you have redeemed us from the curse of the law, having become a curse in our place.

Father, I confess all my sins; the ones I know about, and the ones I have not recognized. I am sorry for them all. I ask You to forgive me and cleanse me with Your precious blood.

Father, the law says that You will punish the sins of our forefathers down to the third and fourth generations. So I now repent of all the sins from my family line, and I ask You to forgive and cleanse me from all the effects of those sins. You promise in Your Word that whoever calls upon Your name will be delivered. I call on You now in the Name of Jesus, to set me free.

Now Satan, I say to you, you have no right to me. You have no right to my house or property. You have no right to my family, nor anything else that belongs to me. I take authority over you. In the mighty Name of Jesus and by the power that is in His blood, I command you to get out of my life. Every inherited curse is leaving now, in Jesus Name.

In the Name of Jesus, inherited curses passed down through our families, where there was sexual transgression, where there was incest, where there was abuse; I command it to go. Any generational curses that have arisen due to idolatry, involvement in the occult, false religions or cults, or superstition; I command every one of you to go. Where there were fortune tellings; divination; worship of the sun, moon or stars; or various types of astrology, I command every one you spirits to go now, in the power of the Name of Jesus. Where there was praying to the dead, Mariology, or necromancy, we command you to go in Jesus Name. Where there was bowing down to images, we command that legal right over us to be broken in Jesus' Name.

That is not our inheritance. We are walking in the truth and in the light. We are walking in the presence of God. All you evil forces must go now.

You spirits that bring hindrance to our walk with the Lord, that hinder us from reading our Bibles or getting anything out of our Bible readings; you spirits that hinder us in our prayer life and fill our lives with all sorts of distractions, in the Name of Jesus we command every spirit of hindrance and distraction to go now! You spirits that hinder the move of the Holy Spirit, and that hinder the flow of the gifts of the Spirit, or that hinder us from hearing clearly the voice of God, I command you to go now in the mighty name of Jesus.

We are set free now to be the people God created us to be. Our homes, our properties and our families are set free from demonic harassment by poltergeist spirits. And we rely now on the precious Holy Spirit to reveal to us in His still, small voice, anything that is spiritually wrong in our house or property, that we might fully cleanse ourselves from the works of darkness, in Jesus Name.

Amen!

FRANK HAMMOND BOOKS & EBOOKS

PIGS IN THE PARLOR   0892280271

A handbook for deliverance from demons and spiritual oppression, patterned after the ministry of Jesus Christ. With over 1 million copies in print worldwide, and translated into more than a dozen languages, *Pigs in the Parlor* remains the authoritative book on the subject of deliverance.

STUDY GUIDE: PIGS IN THE PARLOR   0892281995

Designed as a study tool for either individuals or groups, this guide will enable you to diagnose your personal deliverance needs, walk you through the process of becoming free, and equip you to set others free from demonic torment. Includes questions and answers on a chapter-by-chapter basis as well as new information to further your knowledge of deliverance.

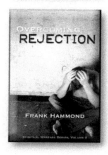

OVERCOMING REJECTION   0892281057

Frank Hammond addresses the all-too-common root problem of rejection and the fear of rejection in the lives of believers, and provides steps to be set free. Learn how past experiences can influence our actions, and how we can be made whole.

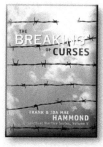

THE BREAKING OF CURSES   089228109x

The Bible refers to curses more than 230 times, and 70 sins that cause curses are put forth in Scripture. Learn how Curses are just as real today as in Biblical times. This book shows what curses are and how you may deliver yourself and your family from them.

A MANUAL FOR CHILDREN'S DELIVERANCE   0892280786

The Hammonds' book for ministering to children is a valuable tool for parents to learn how to set their children free from spiritual bondages. Learn the basics of how to effectively minister deliverance to children.

FRANK HAMMOND BOOKS & EBOOKS

CONFRONTING FAMILIAR SPIRITS 0892280174

A person can form and develop a close relationship with an evil spirit, willfully or through ignorance, for knowledge or gain. When a person forms a relationship with an evil spirit, he then has a familiar spirit. Familiar spirits are counterfeits of the Holy Spirit's work.

REPERCUSSIONS FROM SEXUAL SINS 0892282053

The sexual revolution has impacted our nation, our church and our family. Promiscuity, nudity and sexual obscenities have become commonplace. The inevitable consequence of defilement is the loss of fellowship with a holy God. Learn how to break free from the bondage of sexual sin.

THE MARRIAGE BED 0892281863

Can the marriage bed be defiled? Or, does anything and everything go so long as husband and wife are in agreement with their sexual activities? Drawing from God's emphasis on purity and holiness in our lives, this booklet explains how to avoid perverse sexual demonic activity in a home.

SOUL TIES 0892280166

Good soul ties covered include marriage, friendship, parent/ child, between christians. Bad soul ties include those formed from fornication, evil companions, perverted family ties, with the dead, and demonic ties through the church. Learn how you can be set free from demonic soul ties.

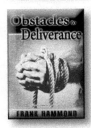

OBSTACLES TO DELIVERANCE 0892282037

Why does deliverance sometimes fail? This is, in essence, the same question raised by Jesus' first disciples, when they were unable to cast out a spirit of epilepsy. Jesus gave a multi-part answer which leads us to take into account the strength of the spirit confronted and the strategy of warfare employed.

THE PERILS OF PASSIVITY 089228160X

Some have made deliverance their ultimate goal in life. Deliverance is not a final goal, it is only a sub-goal on the way to fulfill God's purpose in life. God said to Pharaoh, "Let my people go that they may serve Me..." (Exod. 7:16). There is a purpose in God for each of us - and it is not passivity! Passivity is a foe – it will even block deliverance.

KINGDOM LIVING FOR THE FAMILY   0892281006

God has a specific plan for your family, one that includes the peace, joy, and righteousness of the Kingdom of God. However, too many families have settled for much less than what God has to offer. Gain insights into the root causes of common problems in marriage, spiritual warfare in the family, scriptural guidance on the roles of husbands and wives, bringing up children in the Lord, and more!

FORGIVING OTHERS   089228076X

Unforgiveness brings a curse, and can be a major roadblock to the deliverance and freedom of your soul. Find the spiritual truths regarding the necessity of forgiveness and the blessings of inner freedom which result! Find out why "70 times 7" is for our benefit as much as for the people we forgive.

THE SAINTS AT WAR   0892281049

The Hammonds' book on waging spiritual warfare over territories, including families, churches, cities and nations. Learn about warfare in the heavenlies, and how to pray to change history and fulfill the Great Commission.

PROMOTED BY GOD   089228093X

How did Frank Hammond receive his powerful anointing to minister healing and deliverance for the Lord? Find out in his personal testimony, Promoted by God. Also, find answers to the questions: Is the Baptism in the Holy Spirit for today?, What was the purpose of this baptism? What were the qualifications for it? Were tongues a part of this experience? Did tongues have any useful purpose?

THE FATHER'S BLESSING   0892280743

The body of Christ is missing out on something of great significance - The Father's Blessing. And yet the Patriarchs of the Old Testament (Abraham, Isaac, Jacob) all practiced it. The effects of such a blessing are far reaching, and can readily make the difference between success & failure, victory & defeat, happiness & misery.

Do Your Relationships Produce
Bondage or Joy?

Does someone manipulate you?
What are the symptoms of an ungodly relationship?
Are you tormented with thoughts of a former lover or friend?
Are you free to be all that God intended you to be?

9780892281398

STUDY GUIDE 9780892282043

"Here at last is a thorough and theologically sound treatment of a little understood subject" - from the *Foreword* by Frank Hammond

Breaking Unhealthy Soul-Ties
by Bill & Sue Banks

Unhealthy soul-ties involve the control of one individual over another, and can be one of the most difficult blocks to spiritual freedom. Some relationships are healthy and bring blessings into our lives; other types of relationships can bring demonic bondage to our souls. This book assists the reader in diagnosing both healthy and unhealthy relationships, and offers positive steps to personal freedom.

Miraculous Testimonies
of Spiritual Warfare!

089228031X

POWER FOR DELIVERANCE - THE SONGS OF DELIVERANCE
BY BILL BANKS

This **book,** or **e-book**, shows that there is help for oppressed, tormented, and compulsive people, and that the solution is as old as the ministry of Jesus Christ. From over 30 years of counseling and ministering deliverance, in the United States and abroad, Bill Banks highlights the common root causes of emotional and mental torment, and walks the reader through steps to be set free. Read numerous case studies of people who have been delivered from their torments and fears, including testimonies of over 60 spirits...

Drugs	**Anger**	**Cancer**	**Pornography**	**Perversion**
Fears	**Harlotry**	**Hatred**	**Witchcraft**	**Rebellion**
Cocaine	**Rejection**	**Temper**	**Occult Spirits**	**Childlessness**
Terror	**Torment**	**Suicide**	**Disobedience**	**Unforgiveness**
Smoking	**Murder**	**Bitterness**	**Foolishness**	**Abuse**

Sleeping Disorder & more!

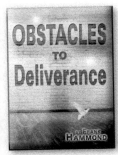

Other Books & E-Books By Frank Hammond

9780892283682

THE DISCERNING OF SPIRITS

We are equipped by God for spiritual warfare through the gifts of the Holy Spirit mentioned in 1 Corinthians 12. God has said that these are the channels through which His power will flow, the avenues through which His Holy Spirit will operate. Chief among these gifts for the ministry of deliverance is the gift of the *discerning of spirits.* Frank Hammond explains the application of this gift to the believer, and provides examples of how it has worked in his own ministry.

PRAISE: A WEAPON OF WARFARE & DELIVERANCE

Praise is a powerful weapon in deliverance and spiritual warfare. As you praise the Lord, things begin to happen in the unseen realm. When Saul was troubled by an evil spirit, the only thing they knew to help him was to call David. When David began to play on his harp and sing praise to his God, the evil spirit departed from King Saul. A demon cannot exist in that atmosphere — he simply cannot function.

9780892283859

9780892283842

SPIRITUAL WARFARE FOR LOST LOVED ONES

Through spiritual warfare, intercessory prayer, and the ministry of love, we are able to help create the best possible environment around a loved one to come to know Jesus. But we must not lose our closeness with the Lord in the process, as these situations can be quite challenging to our spiritual walk. Frank Hammond says, "Don't let your family or friends go without resistance. Get in the spiritual battle, fight for your loves ones!"

Impact Christian Books

Website: www.impactchristianbooks.com

Phone Order Line: **(314)-822-3309**

Address: **Impact Christian Books
332 Leffingwell Ave. Suite #101
Kirkwood, MO 63122 USA**

Lightning Source UK Ltd.
Milton Keynes UK
UKHW020645180321
380569UK00011B/626